From FLOWER to FLOWER

From FLOWER to FLOWER
Animals and Pollination

Text by PATRICIA LAUBER   Photographs by JEROME WEXLER

Crown Publishers, Inc. New York

Photo Credits

Jacket photo and p. 22, hummingbird © Len Rue, Jr., Photo Researchers, Inc. Jacket photo and p. 20 © Bruce Hayward. P. 3, daisy © David Scharf, Peter Arnold, Inc.; Kentucky blue grass © Phil Harrington, Peter Arnold, Inc.; marigold © David Scharf, Peter Arnold, Inc.; coleus © David Scharf, Peter Arnold, Inc. Pps. 20–21 © Bruce Hayward. Top photo p. 22, © U.S. Department of Agriculture photo. P. 22, © Len Rue, Jr., Photo Researchers, Inc. P. 42, © J. M. Comrader, National Audubon Society, Photo Researchers, Inc.

Published by Crown Publishers, Inc., 225 Park Avenue South, New York, New York 10003,
and represented in Canada by the Canadian MANDA Group

CROWN is a trademark of Crown Publishers, Inc.
Manufactured in the United States

Library of Congress Cataloging-in-Publication Data
Lauber, Patricia.
  From flower to flower—animals and pollination.

  Summary: Text and illustrations describe the many ways that flowers are pollinated with
emphasis on the role of bees in this important process.   1. Pollination—Juvenile litera-
ture.   2. Flowers—Juvenile literature.   [1. Pollination.   2. Flowers.   3. Bees] I. Wexler,
Jerome, ill. II. Title.
QK926.L38   1986   582'.0166   86-4566
ISBN 0-517-55539-5

10 9 8 7 6 5 4 3 2 1

FIRST EDITION

Contents

Honeybees at Work

Bees find food in flowers. That is why you are likely to see bees wherever flowers bloom—in fields, orchards, parks, gardens, along the sides of roads. The bee on this apple blossom is a honeybee.

Honeybees live in large colonies, which may have 30,000 to 80,000 adult bees. Each colony has a queen, a big female bee. It also has several hundred male bees, called drones. Once the queen has mated with several of the drones, she spends her time laying eggs, as many as 1,500 a day.

Most of the bees in the colony are small females that cannot lay eggs. These are worker bees. They do all the work of the colony; the drones do none. Some worker bees feed the queen. Some clean the hive. Some guard it. Some make or repair honeycombs, where honey is stored and the queen lays her eggs. As the young hatch out, some workers take care of them and give them food. Still other workers keep making trips out of the hive to find food and bring it back.

Worker bees find two kinds of food in flowers. One is the fine powdery dust called pollen, which you see in this magnified photograph of a portulaca flower. Most pollen is yellow, but some kinds of flowers have white, red, blue, or black pollen.

DAISY

KENTUCKY BLUE GRASS

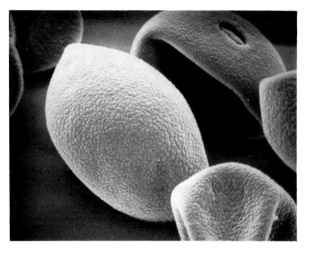

Pollen grains are tiny. Yet each kind has its own shape, as you can see in these photographs of magnified grains.

MARIGOLD

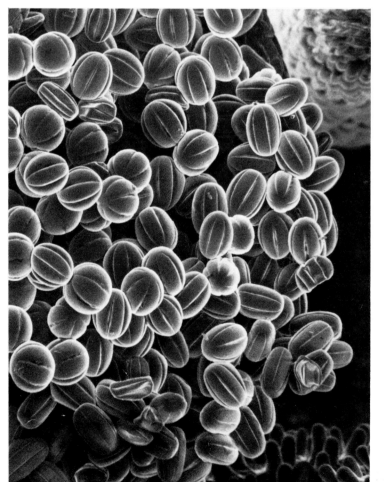

COLEUS

3

Many flowers also make a sweet, sticky liquid called nectar, which is mostly a mixture of sugar and water. Nectar is the raw material from which bees make honey, and it is their second flower food. Adult bees feed on nectar and sometimes on pollen. The young feed on honey and pollen. Pollen is rich in protein, fats, minerals, and vitamins, which the young need in order to grow.

All the honeybees you see on flowers are workers. They visit flowers to collect food. They must gather enough to feed the colony in warm weather. They must also gather enough to feed the colony in colder weather, when there are no flowers.

If you watch honeybees at work on flowers, you will see how they collect and carry pollen. (*Warning: Do not go too close. Bees may sting.*)

Like all bees, workers have six legs, wings, hairy bodies, and feelers. At first glance it does not seem as if they could carry anything. But they can. Each worker has two hairy baskets on her hind legs. They are where she stores the pollen.

Each hind leg has a kind of comb. The bee uses the combs to collect the masses of sticky pollen.

To collect pollen, a worker moves from flower to flower. At each flower she scrapes off pollen with her legs and mouth parts. Still more pollen sticks to her body hairs. Sometimes she has pollen all over her body.

From time to time, the bee cleans herself and arranges her pollen. She may do this while resting on a flower, hovering in the air, or flying from one flower to another. Her legs are lined with stiff hairs, which serve as brushes. The bee uses them to collect pollen from her body.

She uses her mouth parts to moisten the pollen with a little nectar she has collected. The nectar makes the pollen sticky.

6

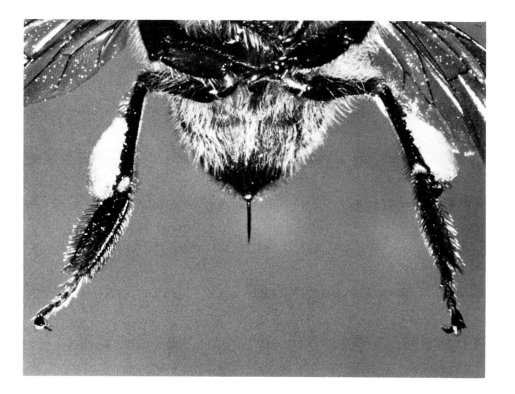

Just above the comb, each hind leg also has a pollen basket made of stiff hairs. The bee scrapes one hind leg down against the other, forcing pollen into the basket on the moving leg.

Then she does the same with her other leg. Now she is ready to go on visiting flowers. When both baskets are full, she flies back to the hive, carrying a large mass of pollen on each hind leg. She leaves the pollen at the hive with other workers, and flies out to collect more.

Worker bees also collect nectar. Because nectar is a liquid it cannot be carried in a basket. Instead, it is carried in a special stomach called the honey stomach. The honey stomach lies in front of the stomach that digests the bee's own food.

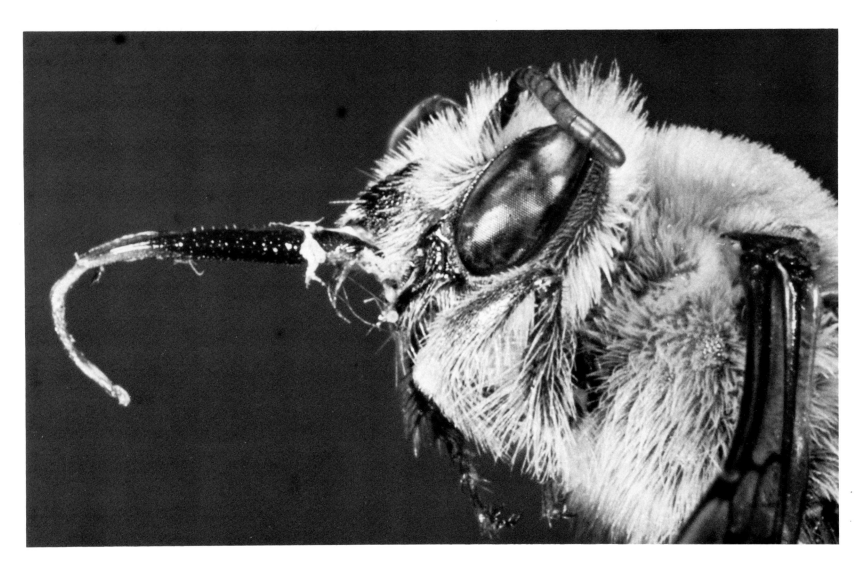

A honeybee has a long tongue that is shaped like a tube. She sticks out her tongue to suck up nectar. The nectar is pumped into the honey stomach. There, as the bee flies around, a chemical change takes place and the nectar starts to become honey.

The worker keeps visiting flowers and collecting nectar until she has a full load. Then she flies back to the hive. She brings up the nectar, much as birds bring up food to feed their young. By this time the nectar is like watery honey. It is received on the tongues of other workers. They work it with their tongues and fan it with their wings to make the water evaporate. The nectar thickens into honey.

While collecting nectar, a worker often picks up pollen on her body. Sometimes she packs it into her pollen baskets. Other times she seems not to want it and gets rid of it in flight.

Collecting food is a big job, and the worker bees work very hard. A honeybee colony uses 50 to 75 pounds of pollen each year. Every grain of this must be gathered by worker bees and carried into the hive. It takes about 38,000 collecting trips to carry 1 pound of pollen to the hive. A trip can be short if a bee is visiting flowers that are rich in pollen. Usually, though, a bee must visit many flowers to gather a full load.

Once a worker starts to collect food, she does not live long. She works herself to death in about 14 days, dying at the age of 5 or 6 weeks. But other workers are ready to take her place.

10

Flowers at Work

Flowers make the food that bees need. As the bees collect it, they do something that flowers need. They help flowers make seeds without knowing it. Bees and flowers fit together like pieces of a puzzle. The bees could not live without the pollen and nectar of flowers. Without bees, many kinds of flowers could not make the seeds from which new plants grow.

Making seeds is the work that flowers do. It is done by their male and female parts.

The female parts make egg cells. These look like tiny seeds, but they are not. Nothing can grow from them. Egg cells are seeds-to-be. The egg cells in this daffodil are at the base of the flower.

The male parts of flowers form pollen grains.

Before an egg cell can become a seed, it must be joined by the content of a pollen grain from the same kind of flower. That is, the egg cell must be fertilized.

As time passes, flower petals fade and dry up. Other parts of the flower also wither away. But the part that holds the seeds keeps growing. This part is called the fruit. Some fruits are kinds you eat, such as cherries or squashes, but most are not. A fruit is simply the flower part that holds the seeds.

Some flowering plants can make seeds without outside help. A tomato plant is one of these. A tomato flower makes egg cells and pollen grains at the same time. The ripe pollen grains fall on the tip of the female part of the flower. Once this happens, you can say pollination has taken place or that the flower has been pollinated.

Each pollen grain grows a tube that reaches an egg cell. Material from the grain travels along this tube and fertilizes the egg. In the days that follow, the flower parts fall away, but the fruit goes on growing. It becomes a tomato.

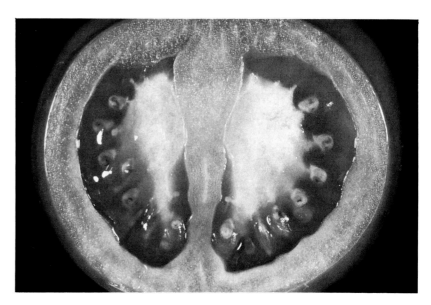

Some other flowers also pollinate themselves. Garden peas, lima beans, soybeans, and peanuts all do. So do the flowers of green beans. Once the egg cells have been fertilized, the fruit starts to grow and it becomes a green bean, as you can see in these photographs.

Many flowers cannot pollinate themselves. For example, certain kinds do not have both male and female parts. They have one or the other. The female parts need pollen grains that come from other flowers of the same kind. So do all flowers that cannot pollinate themselves.

Flowering plants cannot move around the way animals do. They need help if pollen is to travel from one flower to another of the same kind.

Some, like this white birch, have the wind as a helper. The flowers of each plant produce millions of tiny, light grains of pollen. When the wind blows, it carries off the pollen. Much of the pollen is lost. It falls on the ground, in water, on the wrong kind of flower, or in some other place where it is wasted. Still, these flowering plants produce a huge amount of pollen. They make so much that some grains do fall on the same kind of flower, sometimes many miles away. The wind helps to pollinate the flowers of oak trees, grasses, cattails, ragweed, and many other plants.

Corn is one of the plants known as grasses, and it is pollinated by wind. In corn, pollen forms in the branched tassel at the top of the stalk.

The egg cells are in the ears, which have silk growing out of them. Each silk is attached to an egg cell.

The pollen grains are held in little sacs that grow along the tassel. Each sac has a small hole at its lower end. The hole is so small that you need a magnifying glass to see it. When the wind blows, pollen is shaken out of the hole, like salt from a shaker. Wind carries the pollen away from the corn plant. Some of it may land on the silk of other corn plants.

A grain of corn pollen sends out a threadlike tube that grows down through the silk toward the egg cell. Material from the pollen grain travels down the tube and fertilizes the egg. Each fertilized egg cell becomes a kernel of corn.

Many flowering plants are pollinated by insects and other small animals that find food in flowers. The animals usually have wings and can fly quickly from one flower to another, instead of having to crawl up and down stems or tree trunks. And they usually have hairs, feathers, or scales to which pollen sticks. As they visit flowers, their bodies pick up pollen. When they fly to other flowers, some of the pollen rubs off on the female parts of those flowers. If the flowers visited are all the same kind, they are pollinated.

Some Animal Helpers

A few kinds of bats find food in flowers. Most of them live in the tropics, where flowers bloom all year round. But some travel to other regions for part of the year. In late spring, for example, long-nosed bats start arriving in southern Texas and Arizona for the summer.

This small bat has a long muzzle and a long tongue. The tongue is covered with little bumps that act like bristles on a brush. A long-nosed bat uses its tongue to take nectar from the flowers of desert plants. As it does so, pollen sticks to its fur and is carried on to another plant.

Long-nosed bats are active at night, and they feed at flowers that open at night, such as the flowers of the shin-dagger plant. These flowers grow on a tall stalk. A bat may land at the top and work its way down, feeding at each flower along the way. Or it may fly toward a flower, brake in front of it, feed in an instant, and fly on.

Flowers of the saguaro cactus are big and deep. A bat may stop in flight to feed. Or it may grasp the petals and force its small body into the open flower. The bat is so gentle that it does not harm the flower.

When a long-nosed bat feeds at a flower, its head becomes dusted with pollen. Some brushes off on the next flower it visits.

Some kinds of birds also find food in flowers. Like the bats, most of them live in the tropics, but a few visit other areas. One of these is the white-winged dove, which arrives in the Arizona desert just as the saguaro flowers start to bloom. A dove drinks nectar by dipping its bill into an open flower (top photograph). As it does so, pollen sticks to its feathers and is rubbed off on the next flower it visits.

Cactus wrens, thrashers, Gila woodpeckers, and gilded flickers also visit saguaro flowers. So do moths and bees. The saguaro needs many visitors because it blooms for only a short time. A saguaro flower opens one evening, sometime between sunset and midnight. It closes the next afternoon. During these few hours, pollination must take place if the flower is to make seeds.

Outside the Arizona desert, hummingbirds are the only birds that pollinate flowers in the United States and Canada. A hummingbird is tiny. It hovers in front of a flower by beating its wings in the air (bottom photograph). It sips nectar, then flies on to the next flower, carrying pollen on the feathers of its head.

22

Most flowers are pollinated by insects. Butterflies and moths are two of the most important.

If you watch butterflies, you can see what they do. They are active by day and they like bright flowers. They also like to rest while they feed, and so they usually land on flowers.

A butterfly has a long, slim feeding tube. It carries the tube coiled up and out of the way when it is in flight. When it lands to feed, it uncoils the tube. A butterfly feeds by sticking its tube into a flower and drinking nectar. When it leaves a flower, it carries away pollen. Some may be on its feeding tube and some may have stuck to the scales of its body.

Some plants, such as white clover, have many tiny flowers clustered together in a flower head.

If you watch a butterfly feeding at such flowers, you will see something interesting. The feeding tube bends like a knee. Because it bends, the butterfly can move it from flower to flower while resting in one place. The butterfly does not have to spend energy moving around.

Moths are close relatives of butterflies. Like butterflies, they feed on nectar, sipping through a long, slim feeding tube. A moth also coils up the feeding tube when not using it. As a moth feeds, it picks up pollen on its tube or scales. The pollen travels with the moth to the next flower.

Unlike butterflies, moths do not land on flowers. They hover in front of flowers while feeding. Moths are active at twilight or at night, and the flowers they feed at are usually white or pale in color. Most of them give off strong scents that attract the moths.

Certain wasps, flies, beetles, and other insects also pollinate flowers. But of all insects, bees are the chief helpers of flowering plants. Other insects may visit flowers and feed. Bees are the only ones that collect food for themselves and for their young.

Besides the honeybees, there are bumblebees. These big bees have heavy bodies and bright markings of black and yellow or black and white, as you can see in this photograph. Bumblebees live in smaller colonies than honeybees, but they too have a queen that lays eggs and workers that gather food. Bumblebee colonies die out before the coming of winter. Only the young bumblebee queens live on. They sleep through the winter and start new colonies in the spring.

Bumblebees and honeybees are known as social bees because they live in groups and share the work of the colony.

Most kinds of bees do not live and work in groups. Instead, each bee lives and works alone. That is why they are known as solitary bees. Each female mates and then makes her own nest, with about 10 cells where she will lay her eggs. She stocks the cells with pollen and nectar as food for her young. She lays one egg in each cell and seals off the cell. She dies before the young hatch out.

There are many, many kinds of solitary bees—about 17,000. They make up 85 percent of all the kinds of bees in the world. Large numbers of solitary bees may live in one area. They pollinate many wildflowers. They also pollinate crops.

Of all the bees, honeybees may be the busiest. Only honeybee workers need to gather a year's supply of food for their colonies. As they collect this food, they pollinate many flowers. They are also good helpers because they are likely to keep visiting the same kind of flower. If you watch honeybees, you will see them going from cherry blossom to cherry blossom or pansy to pansy. The pollen on their bodies is seldom wasted. It is almost always carried to another flower of the same kind.

Getting Together

A supermarket has a big sign out front so that people will know what it is. The owners put ads in local papers, telling what they have to sell. They hope that people who want to buy food will come to their store.

Something very much like this goes on in the world of nature. When flowers bloom, they serve as ads to bees and other insects. Flowers are a sign of food, of pollen and nectar, and they attract animals that pollinate them.

Some flowers, like dahlias (above) or lilies (below), have bright, showy petals. These flowers are easy for animals to see and find.

Others have many tiny flowers in a cluster. Queen Anne's lace and dandelions, for example, have many tiny flowers, as you can see with a magnifying glass. But each looks as if it had one big flower.

Some flowers, like honeysuckle, give off a scent when their pollen is ripe. The scent makes them easy to find.

29

Flowering plants use pollen, but they do not use nectar themselves. It is something extra that many flowers produce, and it attracts small animals.

Some flowers have a kind of signpost that points to their nectar. The signpost is a pattern that forms a nectar guide.

Look at the photograph of the pansy and you see what is called the flower's face. These markings are really a nectar guide. Other flowers have different markings.

DEPTFORD PINK

PANSY

MORNING GLORY

MARTYNIA

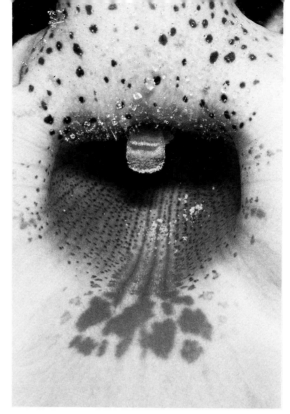

JOHNNY-JUMP-UP

JACK-IN-THE-PULPIT

31

Nectar is usually hidden inside a flower, as you can see in these photographs. The honeysuckle flower has been cut near its base and nectar has leaked out.

With the radish flower, the petals have been removed, leaving the male and female parts. At their base are two shiny drops of nectar.

To reach the nectar in these flowers, a visitor must brush past the male and female parts. Pollen already on its body rubs off on the female part. It picks up pollen from the male parts.

Some flowers store their nectar deep in a spur. In this Johnny-jump-up the spur is the finger-shaped part near the base of the flower. To reach the nectar, a bee, for example, must push its feeding tube into the spur. Pollen already on the tube rubs off on the female part of the flower. As the bee pulls its feeding tube out, pollen grains are jarred loose and stick to it.

In these ways, flowers and insects get together. The size, color, and scent of flowers attract bees and other small animals that are in search of food. Nectar guides may point the way. The animals find food and flowers are pollinated.

But in some flowers, things happen that may surprise you.

More Getting Together

In late spring or early summer the flowers of Japanese barberry open. Look closely at one and you will see two orange marks at the base of each petal. They show where the flower gives off nectar. The female part of the flower is at the center of the petals. The male parts are nestled against the petals.

When a bee reaches for the nectar, pollen on its body rubs off on the female part of the flower. The bee also cannot help touching the male parts. When touched, the male parts snap up toward the center and shower pollen on the bee.

You can make this happen yourself by gently touching the male parts of the flower with a sharp pencil point or a pin. Be sure to choose a flower in which the male parts are lying against the petals. If they are upright, a bee has been there before you.

36

Tiny pouches in the petals hold the pollen-bearing parts of a mountain-laurel flower. When an insect touches them, they snap in toward the center of the flower. The insect visitor is dusted with pollen. In the photograph on the right the flower petals have been pulled back to show how male and female parts look after an insect has visited the flower.

A number of other flowers also dust their insect visitors with pollen. Scarlet sage, or salvia, does something different.

Inside each flower are two levers, or arms, that work like seesaws. The high forward end of each holds the pollen grains. When a bee enters a flower, it passes under these ends. Pushing on toward the nectar, it presses against the lower ends of the levers. The pressure causes the forward ends to swing down and smear pollen on the bee.

The photograph at lower left shows one of the seesaw arms.

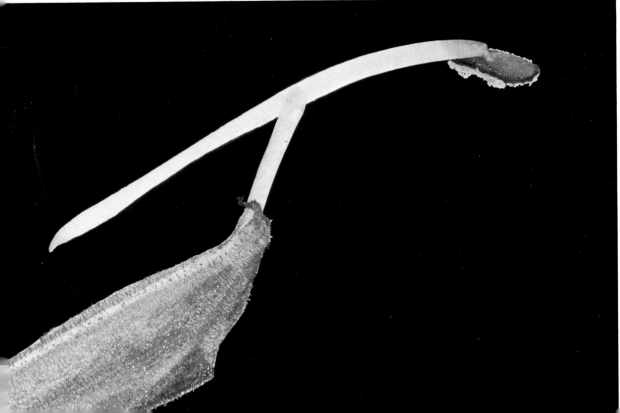

Some flowering plants make very sticky pollen. The grains stick together and form a mass. One of these plants is the butterfly weed.

The tiny flowers of butterfly weed are clustered together in flower heads.

With a magnifying glass you can see that a flower has five parts that look like hoods. The nectar is inside the hoods.

39

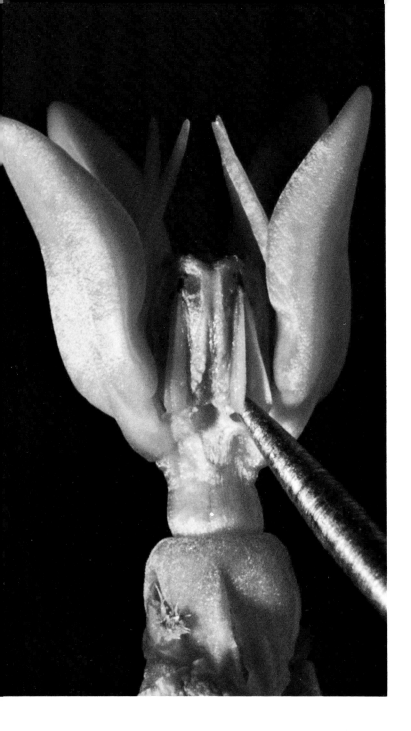

You can also see that there are five slits, each with a tiny black dot at its top. Inside the slits are sticky masses of pollen.

Take a pin—a rough or rusty one will work best. Slip its tip into one of the slits carefully. Lift up gently and the pollen masses will slide out.

You have just done with the pin what a bee's leg does on a butterfly-weed flower. A bee lights on the flower, seeking nectar, but finds the footing slippery. Its leg is likely to slip into one of the slits. As the bee pulls its leg free, it pulls loose the two sticky masses of pollen.

When the bee lands on another butterfly-weed flower, it is likely to slip again. As it tries to free its leg, some of the pollen grains tear off. They fall on a female part of the flower, which is inside the slit.

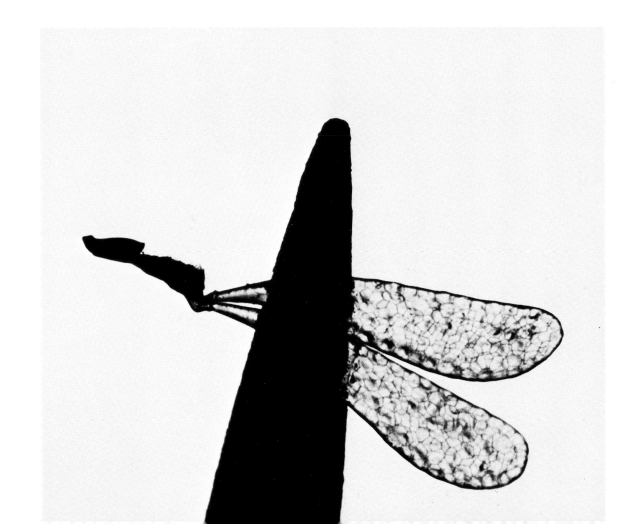

The lady's slipper, or moccasin flower, is a kind of orchid. Like all orchids, it has one petal that is bigger than the others. This petal is called a lip. In the lady's slipper the lip forms a pouch, which looks something like a slipper. When a bee lands on the lip, it faces a large opening. It crawls in to get the nectar inside the pouch. But once in, the bee cannot leave by the same route. There is no room to fly, and the walls of the pouch are too slippery to crawl up.

Searching for a way out, the bee finds a sort of column in the center of the flower. The column is made up of the male and female parts of the flower. At its base are two small openings. To reach one, the bee must first brush past the female part of the flower. Any pollen on its body rubs off. To get out, the bee must squeeze past one of the male parts. Pollen is smeared on the bee's body and carried away to the next lady's slipper that the bee visits.

In northern areas, early spring is chilly. Insects find it hard to warm up enough to fly. Many early-blooming flowers, like the crocus, attract insects because they offer warmth. Their petals form a bowl that catches the sun's heat and reflects it toward the center of the flower. There temperatures may be 10 or more degrees warmer than the outer air. Visiting insects are warmed and the flowers are pollinated.

The skunk cabbage does something else. It makes its own heat. It makes so much heat that it doesn't even have to wait for spring.

In late winter, the skunk cabbage pushes its way up from underground, thawing a path in the frozen marsh and melting the snow above. The plant has a stalk of flowers that look something like a pineapple. They are surrounded by a leaflike hood. The temperature of the outside air may be around freezing. Yet the air inside stays at a steady 72 degrees Fahrenheit during most of the two-week life of the flowers. Scientists think that the flowers and hood serve as a warming hut for insect visitors.

Robbers in the Garden

Flowers have many kinds of insect visitors. Some are looking for mates, some for a place to lay their eggs. Most often the visitors are looking for food. Ants, for example, love sweet foods. They visit flowers for nectar, but they almost never pollinate flowers. Because they are small, ants can usually reach the nectar without touching the pollen. Because they have hard, smooth bodies, most pollen would not stick to them anyway.

An animal like an ant is called a robber. It takes nectar, but it does not pollinate flowers.

A little bit of robbery may not harm a flower. But a flower cannot afford to lose much of its nectar. Then there is not enough to attract the animals that do pollinate it.

Some flowers have defenses against robbers. One of these is the snapdragon. Its petals form a tightly closed pouch. Inside the pouch are the male and female parts of the flower and the nectar. Small robbers cannot get into the pouch. Only a big, strong insect, such as a bee, can. Usually a bee lands on the lower lip of a snapdragon. It forces open the pouch and crawls inside. When it comes out, it is covered with pollen.

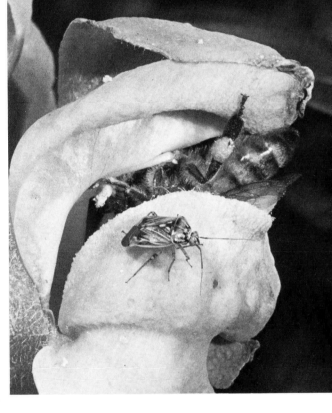

47

Martynia has a stem that is covered with short, sticky hairs. The hairs trap or block robbers that try to crawl up the stem to the flower. Several other kinds of plants, like the catchfly, also have such stems. Still other kinds have such slippery stems that insects cannot crawl up them.

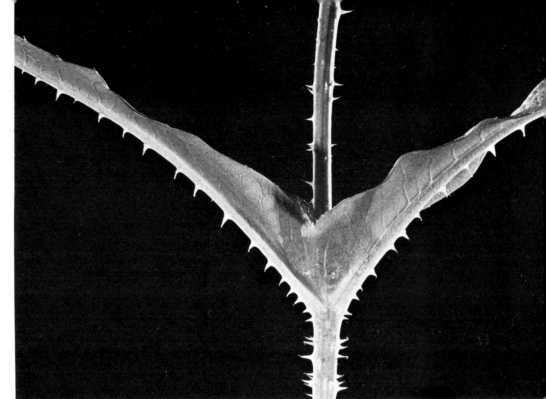

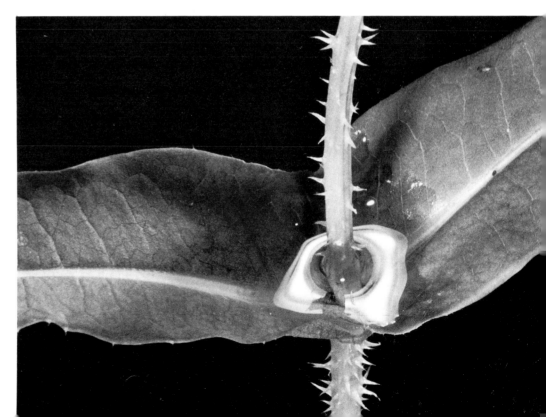

The leaves of teasel grow in pairs. Some pairs are joined at the base, forming a cup. When a cup fills with dew or rainwater, it becomes a moat. The moat blocks small insects that try to crawl up the stem.

Even bees sometimes steal nectar. A bee may bite through the outside of a flower, making a slit. Then it can sip the nectar without going into the flower.

The holes and marks on these blueberry flowers were made by bees stealing nectar.

An alfalfa flower has a little spring in it. When a bee pushes its head into the flower, it triggers the spring. The male parts of the flower pop up and rap the bee on the head, showering it with pollen.

Honeybees seem to dislike being hit on the head. They soon learn not to push into the flower. Instead, they stick their long tongue into the side of an alfalfa flower and steal the nectar.

Most of the time, though, bees gather their food and pollinate flowers at the same time. The bees need the flowers. The flowers need the bees. And all of us need both of them.

The Bee, the Flower, and Me

Alfalfa is used as feed for livestock. It is a big crop and an important one. To raise new crops, farmers need seeds. For seeds to form, alfalfa flowers must be pollinated. Yet honeybees cannot be counted on to do the job. What can farmers do? In the northwestern United States and Canada, they have turned to two other kinds of bees. Both are solitary bees that do not seem to mind being rapped on the head as they collect food. The farmers encourage these bees by creating places for them to nest.

Fruit growers often rent hives of honeybees to place in their orchards when the trees flower. That way they can be sure that there will be plenty of bees to pollinate the flowers—and that fruits will form.

All told, about 90 of our food crops are pollinated by insects, mostly bees. Thanks to bees we have apples, pears, cherries, plums, peaches, and watermelons. We have pumpkins and squashes. We have strawberries, raspberries, and cranberries. We have carrots, cabbages, broccoli, onions. If you add in crops used as feed for livestock, then one third of our food supply somehow depends on flowers that are pollinated by bees.

Bees make honey, which we eat. They pollinate flowering plants that make fruits, vegetables, and feed for livestock, which we also eat. And so, the next time you see a bee on a flower, say to yourself, "The bee, the flower, and me," for like everyone else, you are part of the story of bees and flowers.

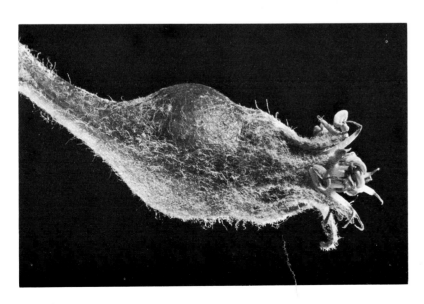

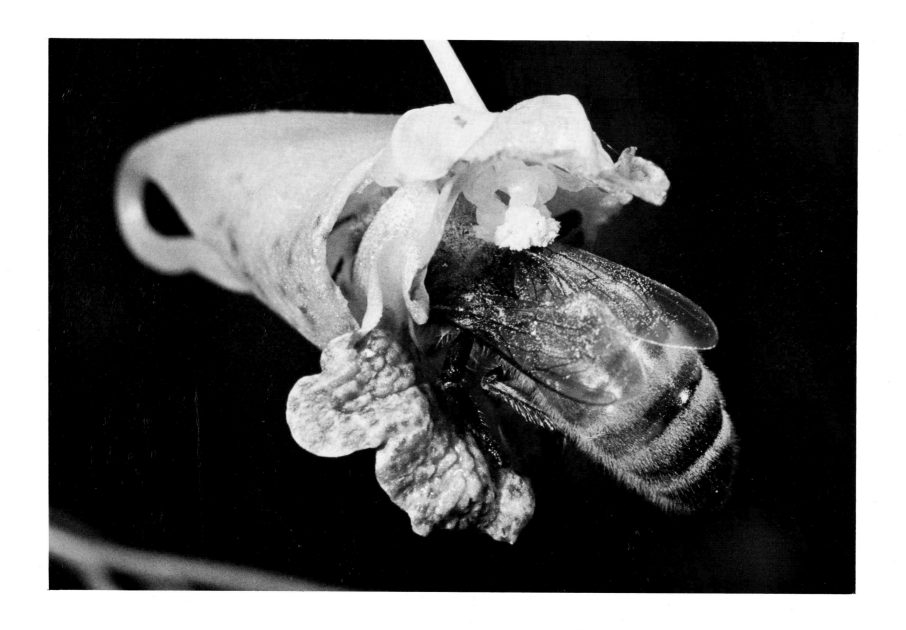

Index